P9-CQJ-302

BELLING THE CAT
AND OTHER AESOP'S FABLES

BELLING THE CAT
AND OTHER AESOP'S FABLES

RETOLD IN VERSE BY
TOM PAXTON
ILLUSTRATED BY
ROBERT RAYEVSKY

MORROW JUNIOR BOOKS/NEW YORK

Inquiries should be addressed to
William Morrow and Company, Inc.,
105 Madison Avenue, New York, NY 10016.

Printed in the United States of America.

1 2 3 4 5 6 7 8 9 10

Library of Congress Cataloging-in-Publication Data
Paxton, Tom.
Belling the cat and other Aesop's fables / retold in verse by Tom Paxton ; illustrated by Robert Rayevsky.
p. cm.
Summary: Selected fables from Aesop include The Night Singer, Honesty Is the Best Policy, and The Milkmaid and Her Pail.
ISBN 0-688-08158-4.—ISBN 0-688-08159-2 (lib. bdg.)
1. Fables. [1. Fables. 2. Stories in rhyme.] I. Rayevsky, Robert, ill. II. Title.
PZ8.3.P2738Be 1990
398.24'52—dc20
[E] 89-39851 CIP AC

To my daughters, Jennifer and Kate
—T.P.

BELLING THE CAT

What a terrible problem the cat was causing—
Eating up all of the mice!
Finally, one of them called a convention.
"Brothers, we need some advice.
Sisters, attention! This cat is a menace—
A threat to us all, through and through.
He'll eat us all if we don't take stern measures.
The problem is: What can we do?"
One mouse stood forth and said, "I have the answer:
This cat is too stealthy, and so
We must tie a great bell 'round his neck, don't you see?
So whenever he nears us, we'll know!"
"Hurrah!" cried the mice.
"What a brilliant solution!
We're saved!" cried the mice.
"We are free!"

They were dancing with joy when a quiet old mouse
Cleared his throat and said, "Please pardon me.
A bell on the cat would be lovely, indeed—
Salvation both timely and fair—
But one thing that worries this old head of mine:
I'm wondering who'll put it there."

Solutions to problems are easy, I vow,
So long as you are not required to show *how.*

THE NIGHT SINGER

A bat was out flying one dark summer's night;
Quite swiftly she hurried along,
When faintly, then stronger, her sharp hearing caught
The air of a beautiful song.
It came from a window, a window thrown open,
And there in the window she heard,
From inside a cage that was yellow and gold,
The song of a musical bird.
"What beautiful music!" the visitor said.
"What heartbreaking music!" she sighed.
"I haven't heard singing so lovely in years!"
"I thank you," the songbird replied.
"Tell me, my friend," said the bat to the bird.
"I don't mean to seem impolite,
But most birds are singing their songs in the sun—
How came you to sing yours at night?"
The songbird sighed deeply and rustled her wings.
"Alas, once I, too, sang all day,
But while I was singing and lost in my song,
Men caught me and brought me away.

You can be certain a lesson was learned—
A lesson I've studied with care:
A bird must be watchful and careful and sharp;
A bird must be always aware."
"Humph!" said the bat. "A lesson well learned,
But one more there needs to be taught:
The time to be careful and watchful, my friend,
Was back then before you got caught!
And so you might add these new words to your song:
Too late to be sorry when things have gone wrong."

TOWN MOUSE AND COUNTRY MOUSE

A field mouse asked a friend of his,
Who lived in a nearby town,
To come and have a meal with him,
But when the two sat down
The town mouse saw their simple fare—
Some barley and some corn—
And said, "You live too poorly here,"
And laughed at the meal with scorn.
"Come visit me," the town mouse cried.
"Pray, come and visit me,
And you'll see true abundance;
You'll see real prosperity."
So off they scurried, off they ran,
Until they came to town,
And there were peas and dates and beans,
And bread both white and brown.

The country mouse was openmouthed:
"Why, look at all you've got!"
He envied all the town mouse had,
And cursed his sorry lot.
But when they'd settled down to eat,
Someone opened the door,
And quick as a flash the two mice ran
Through a chink in the kitchen floor.
When once again the two mice sat
And buttered up some bread,
The door flew open once again,
And once again they fled.

At this the field mouse said, "Farewell.
I'm sorry I did roam.
It's much too frightening living here—
I miss the peace of home.
You seem to have great bounty here,
And yet it costs you dear.
The price you pay is much too high:
Great danger and great fear.
You can't enjoy your wealth," he cried,
"If you're in constant dread.
I'm going home. I much prefer
The simple life instead."

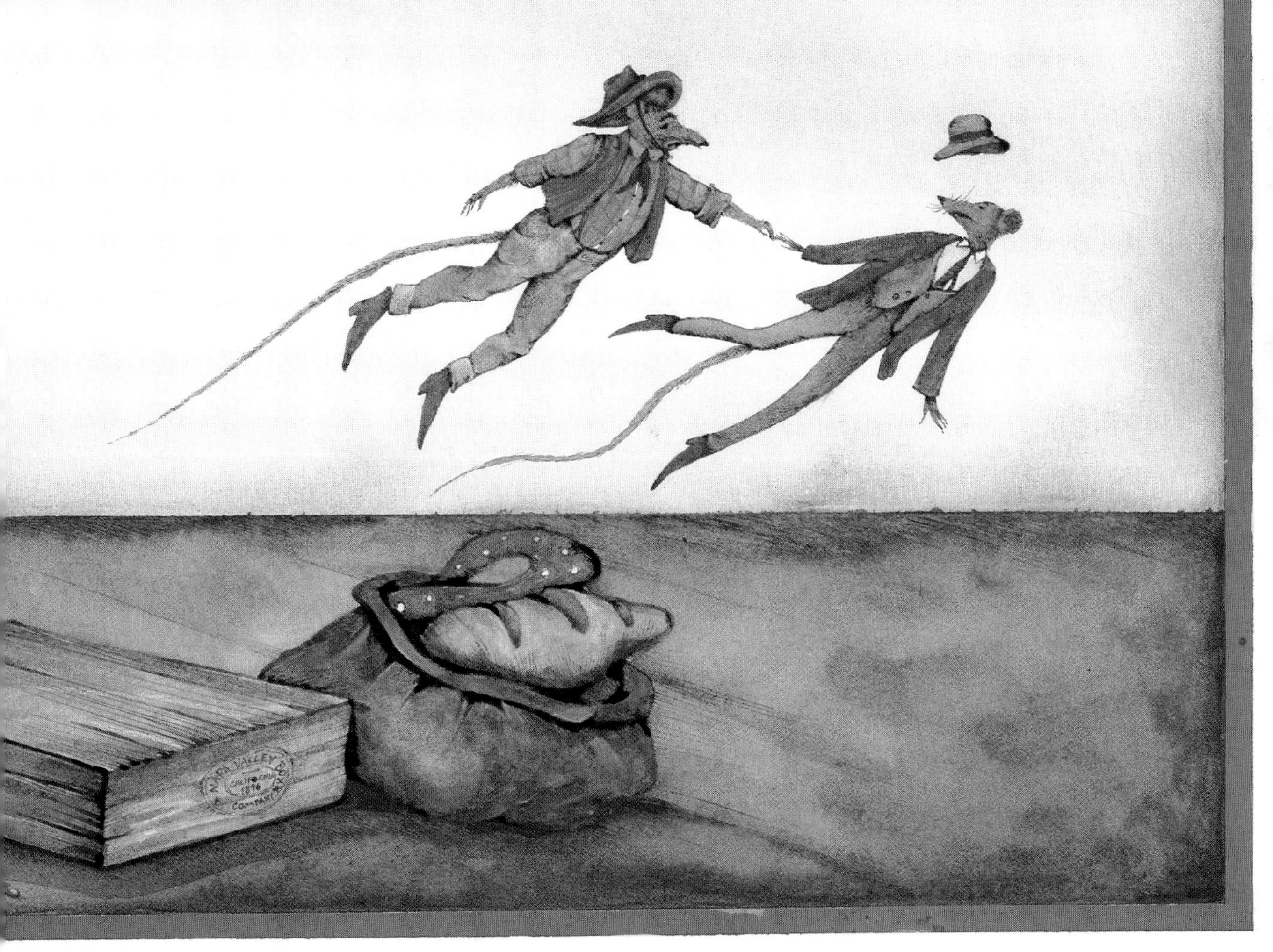

MANY FRIENDS

There once was a hare who had many friends.
So many friends had she,
That she could hardly count them all,
And she was as proud as could be.
But then one day in the forest so green
She heard the most frightening sounds:
Closer and closer the barking and baying,
The noise of a great pack of hounds!

"My friends will soon save me;
I'll run to their side."
She ran to the horse, who said, "Nay.
I've work for my master that has to be done;
I simply can't help you today."
"Nor I," said the bull. "I've appointments elsewhere,
But you'll find assistance—don't fear."
And all of the while the baying grew louder,
The noise of the hounds drawing near!

The goat made excuses, the ram said, "Not I."
The calf said that he was too weak.
At last the poor hare said, "So much for you all!"
And she tore down the road in a streak.
She escaped from the hounds with no help from the rest.
The lesson we're bound to recall:
A person who seems to have so many friends
Often has no *real* friends at all.

THE CROW AND THE PITCHER

"I'm dying of thirst!" cawed the crow in despair.
He looked in a pitcher—some water was there!
He stuck in his beak for a drink, but—hello—
It seemed that the level of water was low.
His beak couldn't reach it,
His chances looked slim,
But then an idea came leaping at him.
He picked up a pebble, flew back in a flash;
It dropped in the pitcher and fell with a splash.
Again and again came the black-feathered flier.
Each pebble that fell brought the sweet water higher.
At last, when the water was near to the brink,
This quick-thinking bird took a well-deserved drink.
So wisdom informs us in this little rhyme,
That little by little will work every time.

HONESTY IS THE BEST POLICY

A woodcutter worked by the side of the river,
Cutting trees on the steep riverbank.
His ax flew out of his slippery hands,
And into the river it sank.
"Oh, no!" he cried. "Without my ax
My chance for a living has died."
He wrung his hands and pulled his hair
And there by the river he cried.
Hermes appeared, this Olympian god,
And when the tale was told,
Took pity and dove to the riverbed
And brought up an ax of gold.

"Is this your ax?" the god inquired.
The honest man said, "No."
A second time the Olympian dove
To the river depths below.
This time a silver ax he found.
"Is this your ax?" again.
"It's not," the woodsman had to say.
"My ax was very plain."
A third time down the brave god dove;
His fortune you can guess.
"Is this your ax, young man?" he asked.
The honest man cried, "Yes!"

And so delighted was the god
(A happy tale I tell)
That he returned the woodsman's ax
And the other two, as well.
The woodsman ran to find his mates,
And when his tale was told,
As proof, he showed his silver ax,
He showed his ax of gold.
One jealous man had this idea:
"I like this little game.
It worked so well for this young man—
I'll go and do the same."
He ran down to the riverbank;
He threw his own ax in;
He kept the one eye open,
As his crying did begin.

Hermes appeared at once to him.
"Why, what's amiss?" he said.
"My ax is gone," the liar claimed,
"And with no ax, I'm dead."
Hermes dove deep. A golden ax
Was proof of his success.
"Is this your ax, young man?" he asked.
Of course, the fool cried, "Yes!"
"You know it's not," the god accused.
The ax sank like a stone.
He not only lost the golden ax;
He also lost his own.

This lesson we must learn in youth:
We're wiser when we tell the truth.

THE BIRD WHO LOST HIS SONG

On a day that is warm,
On a day that is bright,
In a dark chestnut tree
Sits a sorry old kite.
Now the kite is a bird
That is swift on the wing,
But it's well known to all
That a kite cannot sing.
He flies and he dives
And he soars with great skill,
But a kite cannot warble;
A kite cannot trill.

Yet once, long ago,
I can safely attest,
Kites were musical, too—
They could sing with the best.
In choirs, in trios,
In solos they'd sing,
In voices as clear
As a cool mountain spring.
But one day a kite
In a barn full of hay
Heard a great chestnut mare
Throw her head back and neigh.

She made such a sound
That the kite was amazed—
A sound that resounded
Till the poor bird was dazed.
Then, softly at first,
And then louder, the bird
Tried to copy exactly
The sound that he'd heard.
He strove and he strained,
He struggled all day
To sound like the horse
When the horse had gone, "Neigh."

At last he gave up
And decided to sing,
But instead of a song
He sang not one thing.
He tried and he tried,
From sunset to dawn,
But at last the poor kite
Knew his song was quite gone.
He'd foolishly tried
To force out a "Neigh!"
And envy had stolen
His sweet song away.

WHO'S HELPING WHOM?

Who do you suppose was arguing, arguing,
Walking down the middle of the street?
Feet were telling off the tummy pretty well,
And the tummy was sassing back the feet.
Back and forth they were arguing, arguing,
Which was the stronger of the two.
Feet said, "We are. Where would you be
If you didn't have us to carry you?"
"That's all very well," said the stomach to the feet,
"But you need me badly, don't you see?
Without my help you couldn't move at all,
For you get all your strength from me."
How like these squabblers we can be
When we won't join in harmony!
Who needs whom to feel complete?
Feet need the stomach; stomach needs the feet!

THE MILKMAID AND HER PAIL

A farmer's daughter homeward strolled
Late one summer's day.
She'd been to milk the cows and now
She slowly made her way.
As she crossed the rocky fields,
A milk pail on her head,
She fell to dreaming as she walked,
And here is what she said:

"This milk, I vow, will give me cream;
The cream I'll churn to butter,
Which I can take to town to sell."
(Her young heart gave a flutter.)
"With the money I'll buy eggs—
The eggs will hatch, and then
Those chickens will lay other eggs
And still more eggs again!
Till soon I'll have so many birds
I'll take them all to town
And sell them for the money
To buy a silken gown— "

"A dress I'll wear with dancing shoes
When I'm the queen of the ball—"
She tried a little spinning step
And promptly took a fall.
The milk spilled out upon the ground;
It ran away in streams.
So much for all her glorious plans!
So much for her grand schemes!

How often victory's laurels are snatched
When we count our chickens before they're hatched.

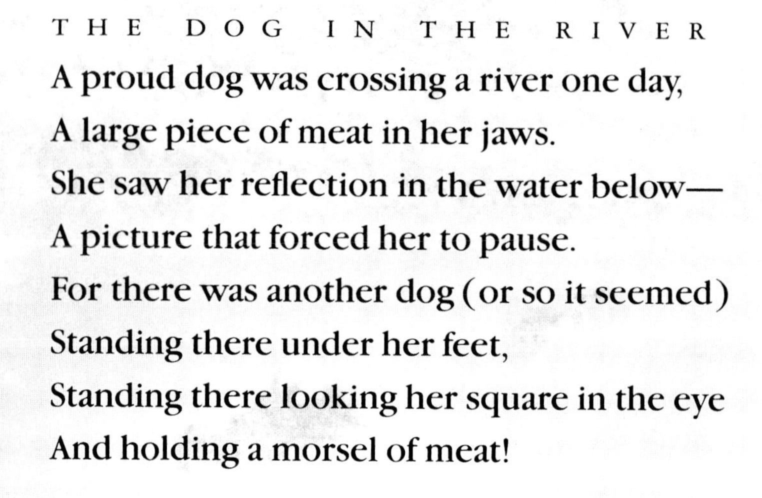

THE DOG IN THE RIVER

A proud dog was crossing a river one day,
A large piece of meat in her jaws.
She saw her reflection in the water below—
A picture that forced her to pause.
For there was another dog (or so it seemed)
Standing there under her feet,
Standing there looking her square in the eye
And holding a morsel of meat!

It seemed so much larger than hers that she sprang
To snatch it away in a flash,
But while she was opening her jaws for the prize,
Her own meat fell in with a splash.
It went with the current;
She saw it no more;
The poor dog crept onto the shore.
She foolishly lost what she already had,
In trying to get something more.

DISCARDED
ANNIE WALLACE